Who Are We?

Who Are We?

Edith Hoisington Miller
Last Poems: 2016 – 2017

Compiled and Edited by
Joel Miller and Keith Helmuth

Chapel Street Editions

Copyright © 2019 by The Estate of Edith Hoisington Miller
All rights reserved

Published by
Chapel Street Editions
150 Chapel St.
Woodstock, New Brunswick E7M 1H4
www.chapelstreeteditions.com

ISBN 978-1-988299-22-8

Library and Archives Canada Cataloguing in Publication

Title: Who are we? : last poems, 2016-2017 / Edith Hoisington Miller.
Names: Miller, Edith Hoisington, author.

Identifiers: Canadiana 20190071400 | ISBN 9781988299228 (softcover)
Classification: LCC PS8626.I4473 W56 2019 | DDC C811/.6—dc23

Cover paintings by Mark Vatnsdal

Book design by Brendan Helmuth

Dedication

For the grandchildren of Edith & Michael Miller—
Lucy, Ella, Liv, and Isaac (1999-2014).

Contents

Foreword i
Preface v
Who Are We? 1
    Centennial— .3
    Mystical Reveilles 9
    Reeds. 11
    A Morning Walk 12
    Swinging at Marlene's 13
    Cirque de Soleil 15
    Weeds in the Sidewalk. 16
    Requiem 17
    Who Are We? 19
    Water Slide: 7th Elegy For Isaac. 20
    Sanctuary of Silence 21
Acknowledgements. 23
About the Author 25
About the Cover Paintings. 27
Afterword 29

Foreword

Everything I know about Edith Hoisington Miller began in the mid 1970s and continues today as I renew my relationship with her through her poetry.

When we met, Edith lived in Sackville, New Brunswick, with her husband, composer and music professor Michael, and their young sons Nate, Joel and Andrew. I had just arrived to teach music at Mount Allison University, and soon found myself a guest in their house on Milner Avenue.

The home was a dynamic performance piece, a work of art that was continually being reinvented, filled with a deep warmth and vibrant creative energy, the sounds of which often issued from several rooms simultaneously. It was loaded with paintings, sculptures, exotic rugs and woven hangings, books, music, and unusual objects d'art. Old sepia photographs in decorative frames revealed the fabulously-costumed young Edith in her heyday as an interpretive dancer, while others showed her as a lover of the wilderness together with her family of origin on their tiny island off the coast of Maine where she spent many a carefree summer.

Edith was the central figure in their home, rock-solid, attired in casual homespun linens, woollens, and crisp cottons, in shades of understated New England beige and ivory, accented with colourful splashes of silk. Her jewels—chunky silver, bronze, leather, framed amber and natural stone—had fascinating histories which she loved to relate.

Her first collection *Crow Impressions and Other Poems* introduced us to the contrasting worlds in which Edith lived her days as a child, as a young adult, and as a young wife and mother. On the one hand, she was caught up in an effervescent whirlwind of dance, music, and art; on the other, the quiet focus of her interior life blossomed within the Quaker tradition.

Afternoons were good times to visit Edith for tea and conversation. The house took on a special gentleness of spirit when Michael was upstairs in the hallway, sitting in his Meditation Chair practicing Transcendental Meditation. "I can't do that, that TM!" Edith confided. "I've tried. I just fall asleep!" Yet in Quaker circles of quietness where I sat with her from time to time, Edith never fell asleep. The residue of those quiet circles found its way into *Crow Impressions*, and they infuse her poems in *Who Are We?*

In this beautiful collection from the last years of Edith's life, the dynamic movement and energy released in the "gush of waves" shot out of a water slide tube, "swinging" at a teenage dance, and the "gallop" and "scoot" of an acrobatic squirrel, is interwoven with a magical quietness— the special holy stillness in which one is but a tiny speck in an indescribably beautiful world.

Edith Miller asks questions—questions about who we are; we, who profess to love this awesome world yet who continue to make violent war, over and over again. She continually compels us to look outside of our "puffed up" human existence, to come to quiet so that we can learn to see, with unclouded eyes, the world that surrounds us. Her poetry reminds us that what is around us is all that we need. With a feeling of urgency, she asks us to open ourselves to it all. We are invited to contemplate the nature of the Quaker quiet circle where those moved to speak, one at a time, may share, listen and release, and communicate with one another. Ordinary things are extra ordinary.

> Who are we?
>
> We think only humans have a soul?
> We need a new sense of "soul."

Edith's poems do not provide answers, but lead us to ask our own questions. This collection of poems may be small, but it is mighty. The poems are a reflection of the person I knew Edith Miller to be: a woman whose personal and poetic field of influence was ignited by an infectious joie-de vivre, informed by her deep love of music, poetry, dance, and nature.

Janet Hammock
Sackville, New Brunswick
February 2019

Janet Thom Hammock, born in Vancouver, holds an Artist Diploma from the University of Toronto, and both Master and Doctor of Musical Arts degrees from Yale University. She has been a university professor of music for thirty-one years. She was appointed Professor Emeritus of Music at Mount Allison University, Sackville, NB, in 2003.

Preface

What is supernatural?
If we think subjectively as well as objectively,
and we are natural beings,
then thinking of the supernatural is only natural.

– Edith's handwritten note from Summer 2017

There are many things I question; one thing I know for sure is that my mother, Edith Hoisington Miller, was pleased with this collection of poems. She wanted to see them published and shared, and made her wishes known to her publisher, Keith Helmuth, and me in the summer of 2017. It seemed like there was all the time in the world to help out with her latest creative project... but then, there wasn't.

What follows here is a little story of poems lost and found, an incomplete "puzzle poem" left behind on her desk, and how my mother's words have opened portals for me to continue to feel her strong presence even in her physical absence.

A Puzzle

On a bright morning in August 2017, I sat in a bit of a daze at my mother's desk in her Fredericton, New Brunswick house, attempting to identify, sort and reassemble pieces of her life. Poems, prose, passwords, and plans left waiting for her to arrive.

Out in the fridge, a birthday cake sat prepared to help celebrate the birthdays of my father and my brother, Andrew. But she died, leaving us with so many emotions we were not accustomed to processing. She would not want a happy day to turn sad, but she was no longer here to lead her small tribe of men through the appropriate social and community rituals. Her manners were always impeccable.

Fortunately, though not unexpectedly, our circle of family, friends, and Friends stepped up to help us navigate those hazy days; so many people, many of them strangers to me, women and men, older and younger, all sharing fond memories of how she had touched their lives, become part of their own stories. Keith reminded me of the poems that Mom had wanted to publish, suggesting we should move forward on that when things settled down.

In the meantime, I was left with some eclectic handwritten musings from the top of her wooden desk, and the challenge of retrieving a recently obsolete email account to her electric desktop. Mom and Dad had recently changed Internet service providers, and had not gotten around to migrating her old emails to their new account. As if by magic, a friend of a friend appeared, willing to help out with the email migration. She'd been acquainted with Mom through Quaker Meeting, and described her as "…a gentle, curious soul who was quietly fierce about her many passions." We sorted out the email issue, and she reintroduced me to words and ideas in a way that made us seem like old friends. Had Mom somehow sent a kindred spirit to me?

Life is spirit.
A loved one who has died
may lie under ground
but his spirit hovers
and continues.

The spirit
we know
will never
leave us.
   — a piece of the "puzzle poem," Summer 2017

A Path

On another day that August, working in my mother's home office, I answered a phone call to confirm her attendance at a New Brunswick Historical Society event taking place in Beaver Harbour near the end of the month — "The Pennfield Colony and the Quaker Legacy." Without hesitation, I explained the situation and asked to take her place. I remembered that my mom had told me also about a meeting that would take place after that event, a meeting to continue and further strengthen the bonds between Quakers and Indigenous People. I remembered my mother being very insistent about getting there. It was important to her. By following her plans and reconnecting with some of her social justice passions, I had the profound and moving experience of literally following my mother's path after she died. I was also reunited with other kindred spirits within the New Brunswick Quaker community, and members of the Peskotomuhkati Nation.

I am continuing to explore in my own musical work different ways to collaborate across political and cultural lines. It feels like a meaningful way to help cultivate peace and friendship with Indigenous People.

Spirit is
the force that creates
all living things and sustains us.

The loved one lost
has lost only
his physical body.

He lives on in memories
of those who know him.
He has eternal life within
the spirit left in us.
  –pieces of the "puzzle poem," Summer 2017

A Personal Relationship

Both my mom and dad always seemed to be creating their own personal versions of spirituality. Coming up with "your own thing" was practically my mom and dad's religion when it came to art, music, dance, writing, and creating their life together, so why not spirituality; my dad with his, "God is a creative force," idea and my mother with her, "Nature is my church," perspective.

Mom had a close, personal relationship with nature, a relationship she valued and enjoyed tremendously. She introduced us to this way of seeing and being, and encouraged us to develop our own relationships with the red mudflats around Sackville, the forest in winter, the sea, the birds, and with all forms of creation. My first love was a river, and then its fish. It had me hooked until my early teen years when girls and the saxophone lured me away. I feel like nature is my church, too. And I've come to feel like communing with nature is a way for me to hang out with Mom.

Nature is my
my church,
Trees in the forest
are my steeples.

But do we need to look up?
Why not look down?
The earth is a sanctuary
carpeted with
ferns so content
they have stuck around for millennia.
Dawn and dusk robins,
crow societies,
doves and sparrows
are my choir.

The sermon comes in
on the whispering wind,
sensed and
mysterious as an oracle.
I awoke today in heaven on Earth,
with new-mown hay
on the farm next-door.
No bottle of Chanel
has such a scent, I'm sure.
     –pieces of the "puzzle poem," Summer 2017

The Poems

In the spring of 2018, both Keith and I returned to my mother's poems and began working on our pledge to publish and share them with you. I hope you enjoy our offering.

As I watch my red-haired daughter, Liv, dancing, I see her grandmother's spirit at play. Love never dies.

Let's read these poems in a loud voice and bring them to life!

Joel Miller
Montreal
February 2019

Joel Miller was born in 1969 in Sackville, New Brunswick. He picked up the saxophone at the age of ten so he could jam with his older brothers Nate and Andrew. He discovered jazz by listening to his mother's record collection. Since moving to Montreal in 1988, he has formed several performance groups, toured internationally, and released eight albums of original compositions. He has received a variety of music awards, included Junos. He holds a master degree in music from McGill University.

Who Are We?

Centennial —

>   remembering 1967, Sackville, New Brunswick

Like a baby blinking in bewilderment,
dropped from the stork
into a strange land,
>   (I am reminded of my mother's
>   original edition of
>   the Fanny Farmer Cookbook
>   with speckles of sauces
>   on yellowed pages,
>   recipes outmoded but
>   fondly remembered by
>   generations of palates),

we enter the small town
that seems to have been
stilled for a century and
follow the parade
of Canada's Centennial.

But now, gone —

the blacksmith
in his listing shop,
a horseshoe on the anvil
for the harness racers,
then from a collapsed shop
travelling with his kit
to far-off stables;

the cobbler,
tall, ruddy, smiling,
hearty host of men
around the pot-bellied stove
accommodating customers;

the harness shop and
its crafters of
leather horse collars
stuffed with marsh grass,
straps adorned with shiny studs;

the box factory,
its simple machinery cutting out
hundreds of cardboard cubes,
containing those studs and buckles
for traditional leather school satchels;

the hardy foundry workers
of cast-iron stoves and fireplaces,
who had no union or
hardhats or special clothing—
one retired worker
could now play his fiddle
whenever he wanted;

the old post office,
another hub for news, gossip,
and the only mail pickup
for the whole town;

the neighbour behind our house,
bringing us newcomers

a fresh-made pie and
flowers from her garden;

the neighbour to our right,
in old age still chopping wood for her stove,
her washing machine with wringer dryer
just bought from Simpsons-Sears;

the Baptist woman,
thinking nothing of lending
a stranger and novice quilter
her quilting frame,
no questions asked;

the dancers —
men were the performers —
doing the Highland Fling and Sword Dance,
with bagpipes;

the supermarket clerks,
bringing groceries to your car,
traffic pausing to let you cross the street;

the couple
in their grocery shop
wrapping butcher paper
around fresh-cut meat and
tying it with a string
unwinding from a ball;

the family doctor,
delivering every baby in town,
including mine, and

with no more pain than by
trendy Lamaze Method;

the mayor,
hosting the New Year's levee,
wearing his chain of office,
taken in my ignorance to be
a wine steward;

the spring ritual of
burning fields
to renew growth
(but not nestlings),
the fire department standing by—
almost like watching fireworks;

the town fire alarm,
blowing a 9:00 p.m. curfew,
in the middle of a piano sonata
at the Conservatory;

the 11:00 p.m. train,
rolling by, rattling our house,
its mournful horn overpowering
the nightly newscast;

the milkman—
just put the sign in the window
bottles of milk,
butter and eggs,
for morning delivery;

the country general store
with rubber boots,

red and black-checked wool shirts,
local beef, and a wheel of cheddar
kept in a cold case, lit only for perusal
and then turned off;

the foundations of houses,
wrapped in fir branches, seaweed, or sawdust —
readied for winter;

the four-party telephone line —
we are told we are lucky
it's not a ten-party;

the accents —
gentle traces of a Yorkshire tongue,
shades of Acadians and Loyalists
and one Black family,
descended from Loyalist slaves,
its matriarch a member of the I.O.D.E.*;

the newborn kittens
being drowned by the owners
as soon as they pop out,
controlling the cat population
in the traditional way;

the summer kitchen,
its use as unfamiliar to me
as the sump pump
all day regurgitating water
and as the composting method,
"just toss your parings
into the bushes," I am told;

the cow, pushed and yanked
onto a truck, travelling to a new stable
to become a milk machine;

the Black Angus bull,
crossing the highway,
coaxed to a fenced pasture by
Michael, a fearless novice.

That Centennial parade was not flanked
by the maple leaf flag—
so new and controversial then
no store carried it.
Maybe the only one in town was
what I, not yet a Canadian,
made of red and white remnants.

I have flown it
these fifty years.

*And now, the 150th year
of the country is being celebrated.
Fifty years from now
at the Bicentennial,
will the past fifty
look just as quaint?
Will the maple leaf flag
be cached in the computer
and only virtually acquired?*

2017

* I.O.D.E— Imperial Order Daughters of the Empire

Mystical Reveilles

Awakening in a strange bed
in transit to a new town,
I was dazed by the reveille of
a flute-like whistle
piercing the early morning—
two short cheerful beeps
like a panpipe harbinger
of an oncoming train
(a memory of the Erie Railroad)—
then a wailing flute
draping itself along the train
like smoke from a cigarette.

On my first morning
in our new house,
spellbound by the reveille of
another flutey whistle—
a shrill fife
puncturing the still air.
Drifting downward,
floating mournfully,
the plaintive note mewled
in a bleating overtone,
sprinkled snowy notes
into the atmosphere,
then dissolved.

I could only lie and muse
on the dawn mystique
until summoned to get up.

Told it was a factory's
wake-up call to its workers
did not diminish my awe
of the exquisite resonance
that vied with the veery thrush
singing its spiraling panpipe
amid tall trees.

Reeds

My brother is Reed,
as are my father, grandfather,
and son.

I walked through cattail reeds
past the millpond spill
long ago with my aunt,
tapped their fluff to stuff into dolls;

boated through thickets
of reed and rice on Silver Lake,
nibbled on a cattail stalk
tasting like limp celery;

saw a bittern, finally,
after a braying *oongk-a-choonk*
betrayed its location
amid a camouflage of reeds;

hiked High Marsh Road dikes
over masses of marsh reeds
an Impressionist mural
come to life;

smelled the springtime marshes
in old judo mats and horse collars
stuffed with marsh grass,
and in the scents of basket shops;

heard music through reeds
of a riveting sax and plaintive oboe,
and tooted my own frail notes
on a crude reed panpipe.

A Morning Walk

A morning walk on
the ridge above the river,
bare arms bathed
in summer air,
sweat coming with the sun,
dew from the fields,
lilacs and hay filling
the senses.

High on a tall tree,
an outline of red against
a white sky through
the lace of dead branches
a cardinal calls,
obscure by distance but
distinct by song.

A runner in tank-top and
stretch pants, panting,
strapped to gadgets
counting calories and
tuned to iTunes,
a teenager texting
on firmly grasped device.

I hold a daisy
gently in my palm.

Can they even hear the *wheep!*
of the elusive great-crested flycatcher?

Swinging at Marlene's

My buddy Joan and I made it
to Marlene's summer cottage party
in the wild woods that hot green day.
We squeezed on bathing suits,
picked our way on a narrow path
through arching, flapping leaves
to the dammed river pond, and
joined friends splashing in the water.

I swam for the other side,
climbed the bank to a great oak with
a long dangling rope,
grabbed it and swung
in a long arc over the water,
let go and with flailing arms and legs
plopped down in the midst
of cheering water-bobbers.

Returning to the beautiful rope,
I perfected my acrobatic stretch,
and, reaching for the sky, flew
almost as far as a cloud—
as if in a dream realized.

Back to the cottage,
we padded across the plain wood,
rag-rugs absorbing our drippings,
to dress and join the party
around a trestle table
scarfing down baloney,
Wonder Bread, beer and Drakes Cakes.

Plump Marlene, sitting on the lap
of chubby, freckled Freddie —
    they made a chortling, teasing pair
    sharing a bottle —
suddenly slid off and sprinted
to an electric organ.

What was an organ doing in the woods?
A former child prodigy
on the organ, on the stage, Marlene
now had her own Hammond organ
in her studio, her sanctum,
and she was really swinging.
She struck up a familiar refrain
sparking spontaneous singing from all.
Geeky Leroy jitterbugged with me,
swinging me into the air,
over his shoulder—
as if going to heaven again.

Cirque de Soleil

You gallop high up the maple,
scoot on slender twigs,
select a branch
with the choicest seeds
before their wings gyrate
to the ground.

You splendid squirrel,
acrobat in the sky,
you dive to a limb,
sweeping it up and down
under your weight
and cluster of leaves.

Your body, fine in gray fur
and white bib, hangs
elongated from the limb
by back claws,
stretches out to clasp seeds
in nimble paws,
to nibble and crunch.

On the porch railing
your magnificent tail
arches over your back,
so perfectly created,
a rudder for balance
or a work of art,
a sylph so diaphanous
the landscape shows through it.

Weeds in the Sidewalk

Skyscraper
thrusts upward
sleek angles
a bird swoops
hits steel
bronze, glass
drops to pavement

Contrail line
a straight streak in the sky bends in the wind
like a spent reed
dissolves into clouds
a pageantry of bunnies,
Jesus, white roses, cirrus surf,
a cat's tossed belly fur—
like a Rorschach test in the sky

Skyscraper
decrepit and sorry
falls to the wreck of the ball
leaves in the barren space
a vapour of memories
and weeds in the sidewalk
like dropped acorns
gyrated maple seeds
drifted puffs of a dandelion,
that all remember and re-create

Requiem

The stained glass church window—
armoured men on caparisoned horses
rearing their round and glossy flanks,
in a traffic jam of thrashing and
churning, like Sambo's tigers into butter.

Pennants and slanted swords thrust high,
the glass tiles alternate in colour—
red of gore with steel glint of sword.
Is this a holy war?
What's holy about it?

The Romantic scenic revolution—
troops dressed in blue or red tuxedos,
spanking white puttees and jaunty hats,
battle ready, and at a signal
striking and slashing at the facing troops.
Even the poor horses are recruited,
though innocent of human designs.
Is this a war for country?
Hasn't patriotism been taken to an extreme?

Enough already!
Haven't we enough unbidden death—
viruses and volcanos,
droughts and pollution,
blood clots and hunger,
bad experiments of naive adolescents?
Aren't there enough victims
youth, parents, orphans?
Need we contrive cruelty as well?

No less are the drab grays and filth of
trenches, strewn with bodies in dead sprawl
and the weary vigilance of the living;
even the colours of blood and bandage
are drowned in the dour landscape.
Thousands commemorate this theatre noir,
make a census of the sheer number
of the dead and relish the drama.
Is there no theatre in the lush growth
of earth's treasures
beyond a mere field of poppies?

There's life in the gray mud ooze
of barnacled mussel shells,
astonishing order in
parallel potato rows and beach surf,
the scent of phlox in fields,
and honeysuckle over a corduroy road,
the suckle and cuddle of a baby.

Superior to the red and glint on glass mosaic—
roses and fresh moss,
the shimmer of cobwebs in dew,
the changing sky and season
are reasons for celebration
and thanks for the glories in life.

Let us come together in a circle,
speaking in turn and sharing
our differences and commonalities,
no one more important than another.
As Barack Obama advises,
"The forces that divide us
are not as strong as
those that unite us."

Who Are We?

With the manual dexterity
of thumbs opposing fingers,
we can write poems and propaganda,
use tools and play pipes.

But chimps can push a stick down a hole
and extract termites.
The male bowerbird can thatch a shelter,
decorate it with red berries
and then perform a feather dance
to attract a mate. If snubbed,
he starts over again in ever more elaborate collages.

Can we secure a prize piece of food
more quickly than a mouse at the end of a maze,
or an octopus at the bottom of a bottle?
A pitcher plant—
not even a mobile being—
can trap a fly for a meal.
A male seahorse can gestate its own baby.

We have the hyoid bone.
We can speak words,
an eloquent Shakespeare soliloquy,
a Gilbert and Sullivan patter song.
Can we communicate with squeaks and squeals,
like whales in a pod?

Do we grieve more than
a dog does for its dead master
or an elephant at the loss of a family member?

Who are we?
We think only humans have a soul?
We need a new sense of "soul."

Water Slide: 7th Elegy For Isaac*

Springing up the steps to the top
of the water slide,
wet hair straggled to the shoulders,
trunks soaked to the knees,
a tall, lanky youth, probably seventeen—
it was Isaac,
or so it struck me.

He would be seventeen now.
Would he still be as lanky,
a taut-muscled freshman,
stretched out to this youth's height,
his shoulders as broad?

At the end of the chute,
whooshing out with waves
churning into the catch basin,
he made a bigger splash
than the other water sliders.

Again and again, as he
eagerly ascended the steps,
I couldn't keep my eyes off him,
this vision of Isaac,
climbing the wet metal treads
and a minute later
shooting out of the tube
on a gush of waves.

---

* "Elegies for Isaac" 1 through 6 are collected in *Crow Impressions and Other Poems* by Edith Hoisington Miller published in 2016. Isaac Miller, a grandson of Edith and Michael Miller, died in 2014.

Sanctuary of Silence

I stopped skiing, stood still and
alone on a ridge,
a speck on a landscape of
profound silence,
surrounded by snow-laden
balsam and spruce,
their swags intact in the stillness.
Even the rabbits and red squirrels
who had left their dainty tracks
under the boughs
seemed to respect the serenity.
It was hard to believe
there could be such a
a sanctuary of pure silence,
and that I had privileged entry.
Even as the day was dimming,
and I had to resume my way,
I was at one with the snow-draped woods.
The singular sound of the skis
softly caressing the snow
did not mar the peace.

Acknowledgements

With deepest gratitude I wish to thank—

Janet Hammock for the heartfelt and insightful Foreword she contributed to this book.

Mark Vatnsdal for the cover paintings that capture the feeling of our family's Ram Island retreat.

Melony McCarthy for helping me put the Preface together. She did the main labour of connecting my notes and folding the pieces of the "puzzle poem" into both my story and the theme of the book. As if by magic, she gave Edith's unfinished poem a coherent place in her published work.

Keith and Brendan Helmuth of Chapel Street Editions for their artists' vision.

When Keith first approached me about Mom's last poems back in August 2017, his simple gesture opened up a world. He invested such love and care into his work on this project, prompting me to think about the joy my Mom always brought into working with words. What fun they must have had during their collaboration on her previous book of poetry, *Crow Impressions and Other Poems*! It occurred to me that he must also really miss playing with ideas and words with her. I can only hope that creating *Who Are We?* with me brought a tiny bit of the sparkle in Mom's eyes back to him, too.

Joel Miller

About the Author

Edith Hoisington Miller was born in 1932 in Ossining, New York. After a brief career in publishing with the McGraw-Hill Book Company and as a freelance compositor, she met and married organist, choirmaster, and composer, Michael R. Miller. The Millers came to Sackville, New Brunswick in 1967 where Michael served as professor of music for thirty-two years at Mount Allison University. After Michael's retirement, the Millers moved to Fredericton, New Brunswick.

Edith Miller was active in a wide variety of community-based art organizations in Sackville and Fredericton. She participated in choral singing, dancing, and creative writing programs. She taught creative movement to children and adults. In addition, she was deeply engaged in social justice work, including alliance building with First Nation communities. She wrote a biweekly column for the Sackville Tribune-Post on environmental, justice, and Indigenous issues. She did publicity writing for arts organizations and contributed articles on the arts, especially on dance, to various publications. Edith is the author of *Crow Impressions and Other Poems* (2016).

Edith was a member of the Writer's Federation of New Brunswick from which she received awards for her nonfiction writing and poetry. She is the mother of three sons, Andrew, Nate, and Joel, all of whom are musicians. Edith was an active member of the New Brunswick Monthly Meeting of the Religious Society of Friends (Quakers).

About the Cover Paintings

Joel Miller commissioned artist, Mark Vatnsdal, to create the paintings of Ram Island scenes reproduced on the front and back covers. Ram Island, off the coast of Maine, has long been a place of summer retreat for the Miller family. It has been owned for generations by Edith's family of origin. Both paintings are oil on canvas.

The painting on the front cover depicts Michael Miller exploring the water's edge of Ram Island, followed by a young family friend. The painting on the back cover is of Edith Miller in contemplation on the rocky beach of Ram Island. The images capture the timeless pleasure of relaxed days spent with family and friends at the seashore, in harmony with the rhythms of nature.

Afterword

Although Edith Miller was always a writer, she took up the composition of poems in her last decades, a time when those who savour the resonance of words often wish to put their love of life and the beauty of the world into a legacy of language.

With the publication of *Crow Impressions and Other Poems* in 2016, Edith did just that. With the publication of *Who Are We?* she has added a further contribution to this great tradition.

In both books, we encounter the unmistakable imprint of the spirit and energy that animated Edith and her creative work. But what has impressed me most as I have worked with her poems and prepared her books for publication, is the recurring presence of family in what she chooses to celebrate. It has been noted that Edith was the centreing presence of her family, but clearly when she came to focus on what mattered most, family was the centreing presence for her.

At the memorial celebrating her life, husband, Michael, and sons, Andrew, Nate, and Joel, formed a combo to play some of Edith's favourite music, including jazz tunes. At the conclusion, they picked up their instruments and continued to play as they proceeded down the aisle from the front of the chapel to the rear.

Michael led with a little dance step, followed by Joel on the sax, Andrew playing the double bass, and Nate with a hand drum.

It was an astounding moment of celebration in the midst of sorrow by those most affected. It was as if the family, in their natural mode of creativity, had made itself into a tangible expression of the spirit in which Edith lived. The effect was utterly transporting; Edith's family had lifted the celebration into communion with an imperishable love of life.

Between her two books, Edith completed sixty-five poems for publication. Although this is a modest number, the amplitude of her work continues to evoke appreciative response from those who discover it.

My thanks to Joel Miller for his enthusiastic coordination of the work it took to create *Who Are We?* The manuscript was yet to be titled when we began preparing it for publication. Joel chose the title from one of the poems. No second thought was needed. It was a perfect fit. I am sure Edith would agree.

Keith Helmuth, Publisher
Chapel Street Editions
Woodstock, New Brunswick
February 2019

www.ingramcontent.com/pod-product-compliance
Lightning Source LLC
Chambersburg PA
CBHW060345080526
44583CB00014B/1068